OFFICIALLY
WITHDRAWN

Joshua Tree Branch Library
6465 Park Blvd
Joshua Tree, CA 92252

My United States

North Carolina

A N N   O.   S Q U I R E

Children's Press®
An Imprint of Scholastic Inc.

Content Consultant

James Wolfinger, PhD, Associate Dean and Professor
College of Education, DePaul University, Chicago, Illinois

Library of Congress Cataloging-in-Publication Data
Names: Squire, Ann, author.
Title: North Carolina / by Ann O. Squire.
Description: New York : Children's Press, an imprint of Scholastic, 2018. | Series: A true book | Includes
    bibliographical references and index.
Identifiers: LCCN 2017028542 | ISBN 9780531231692 (library binding) | ISBN 9780531247204 (pbk.)
Subjects: LCSH: North Carolina—Juvenile literature.
Classification: LCC F254.3 .S68 2018 | DDC 975.6—dc23
LC record available at https://lccn.loc.gov/2017028542

Photos ©: cover: Walter Bibikow/Getty Images; back cover ribbon: AliceLiddelle/iStockphoto; back cover bottom: wbritten/
Getty Images; 3 bottom: Americanspirit/Dreamstime; 3 map: Jim McMahon; 4 right: Kettaphoto/Dreamstime; 4 left: chas53/
iStockphoto; 5 bottom: IrinaK/Shutterstock; 5 top: Fertnig/iStockphoto; 6 bottom: Kagenmi/iStockphoto; 7 top: Peter Nicholson/
Alamy Images; 7 center: Ian Dagnall/Alamy Images; 7 bottom: Jan Walters/Alamy Images; 8-9: Daveallenphoto/Dreamstime; 11:
RickSause/iStockphoto; 12: ESB Professional/Shutterstock; 13: skiserge1/iStockphoto; 14: William Meyer/Alamy Images; 15:
Mark Kostich/iStockphoto; 16-17: Konstantin L/Shutterstock; 19: The Photo Access/Alamy Images; 20: Tigatelu/Dreamstime; 22
right: Pakmor/Shutterstock; 22 left: Atlaspix/Shutterstock; 23 bottom left: chas53/iStockphoto; 23 top left: IrinaK/Shutterstock;
23 top right: Daniel Prudek/Shutterstock; 23 center left: Dorling Kindersley/Universal Images Group/Newscom; 23 center right:
Kettaphoto/Dreamstime; 23 bottom right: Hong Vo/Shutterstock; 24-25: DEA PICTURE LIBRARY/age fotostock; 27: World History
Archive/Ann Ronan Collection/age fotostock; 29: North Wind Picture Archives/Alamy Images; 30 bottom left: SuperStock/Getty
Images; 30 top: English School/Getty Images; 30 bottom right: Classic Vision/age fotostock/Superstock, Inc.; 31 top right:
konstantinks/Shutterstock; 31 top left: Atlaspix/Shutterstock; 31 bottom: LanceKing/iStockphoto; 32: The Granger Collection;
33: Classic Vision/age fotostock/Superstock, Inc.; 34-35: Philip Scalia/Alamy Images; 36: Karen & Ian Stewart/Alamy Images;
37: Robert Alexander/Archive Photos/Getty Images; 38: Steven McBride/Alamy Images; 39: Pacifica/The Image Works; 40
inset: HandmadePictures/iStockphoto; 40 bottom: PepitoPhotos/iStockphoto; 41: Fertnig/iStockphoto; 42 top left: Underwood
Archives/The Image Works; 42 top right: Rue des Archives/The Granger Collection; 42 bottom left: Stephen Chernin/Getty
Images; 42 bottom right: Everett Collection; 43 top: Gai Terrell/Redferns/Getty Images; 43 center right: Juha Lehto/EyeEm/Getty
Images; 43 center left: Dave Hogan/Hulton Archive/Getty Images; 43 bottom left: DFree/Shutterstock; 43 bottom right: Amanda
Edwards/WireImage/Getty Images; 44 top left: fotoMonkee/iStockphoto; 44 top right: Action Sports Photography/Shutterstock;
44 bottom right: EditorialByDarrellYoung/Alamy Images; 44 center left: diane39/iStockphoto; 44 bottom left: LanceKing/iStock-
photo; 45 center: North Wind Picture Archives/Alamy Images; 45 center right: PAINTING/Alamy ImagesAlamy Images; 45 top
right: Rolfo Brenner/EyeEm/Getty Images; 45 center left: Tampa Bay Times/Lara Cerri/The Image Works; 45 bottom: English
School/Getty Images. Maps by Map Hero, Inc.

No part of this publication may be reproduced in whole or in part, or stored in a retrieval system, or transmitted in any form or by any
means, electronic, mechanical, photocopying, recording, or otherwise, without written permission of the publisher. For information
regarding permission, write to Scholastic Inc., Attention: Permissions Department, 557 Broadway, New York, NY 10012.
© 2018 Scholastic Inc.

All rights reserved. Published in 2018 by Children's Press, an imprint of Scholastic Inc.
Printed in North Mankato, MN, USA 113

SCHOLASTIC, CHILDREN'S PRESS, A TRUE BOOK™, and associated logos are trademarks and/or registered trademarks of
Scholastic Inc.

Scholastic Inc., 557 Broadway, New York, NY 10012

1 2 3 4 5 6 7 8 9 10 R 27 26 25 24 23 22 21 20 19 18

Front cover: Chimney Rock

Back cover: Cape Hatteras Lighthouse

Welcome to North Carolina

Find the Truth!

Key Facts

Capital: Raleigh

Estimated population as of 2016: 10,146,788

Nickname: The Tar Heel State

Biggest cities: Charlotte, Raleigh, Greensboro

United States

North Carolina

Everything you are about to read is true *except* for one of the sentences on this page.

Which one is **TRUE**?

T or F North Carolina fought against the Union during the Civil War.

T or F Sir Walter Raleigh was the first Englishman to visit North Carolina.

First in Flight

LAFF 2 DA

NORTH CAROLINA

Find the answers in this book.

Contents

THE BIG TRUTH!

Emerald

What Represents North Carolina?

Cardinal

Many North Carolinians enjoy the beaches on the state's Atlantic coast.

Gray squirrel

This Is North Carolina!

OHIO

N.J.

DELAWARE

WEST VIRGINIA

VIRGINIA

D.C.

KENTUCKY

1

2

3

4

University of North Carolina

North Carolina Museum of Life and Science

WRIGHT

Grandfather Mountain

Blue Ridge Parkway

International Civil Rights Center and Museum

Wright Brothers National Memorial

Mount Mitchell State Park

Roanoke

Albemarle Sound

TENNESSEE

Mountains

WINSTON-SALEM

GREENSBORO

DURHAM

North Carolina State Capitol

Tar

World's Largest Chest of Drawers

RALEIGH

North Carolina State Fair

Pamlico Sound

Appalachian

ASHEVILLE

NORTH CAROLINA

Pee Dee

CHARLOTTE

Neuse

Outer Banks

North Carolina Apple Festival

Gantt Center for African-American Arts & Culture

National Hollerin' Contest

Cape Fear

WILMINGTON

Cape Hatteras National Seashore

SOUTH CAROLINA

0   50
Miles

USS North Carolina Battleship Memorial

GEORGIA

ATLANTIC OCEAN

1 Mount Mitchell State Park

At 6,684 feet (2,037 meters), Mount Mitchell is the highest peak east of the Mississippi River. Surrounded by a state park, the mountain offers visitors hiking, camping, picnicking, and other outdoor activities.

MOUNT MITCHELL
HIGHEST PEAK EAST
OF MISSISSIPPI RIVER
ELEVATION 6684 FT.

N W E S

② Blue Ridge Parkway

This road runs 469 miles (755 kilometers) through North Carolina and Virginia. Often called America's favorite drive, it is famous for its spectacular scenic views.

③ International Civil Rights Center and Museum

Greensboro, North Carolina, was a major center of activity for the civil rights movement of the 1960s. Today, the town is home to a museum detailing the history of the movement.

④ Wright Brothers National Memorial

In 1903, Orville and Wilbur Wright made history with the first successful engine-powered airplane flight. It took place near Kitty Hawk, North Carolina. The brothers chose Kitty Hawk for their test site because of its soft, sandy landing surface and regular breezes.

The Blue Ridge Mountains are named for the blue mist or haze that seems to cover their slopes.

CHAPTER 1

Land and Wildlife

North Carolina is nestled in the southeastern region of the United States. To the south are Georgia and South Carolina, to the west is Tennessee, to the north is Virginia, and to the east is the Atlantic Ocean. With 53,821 square miles (139,396 square kilometers) of land area, North Carolina is our nation's 28th-largest state. But what it lacks in size, it makes up for in the amazing variety of its landscape, animals, and plants.

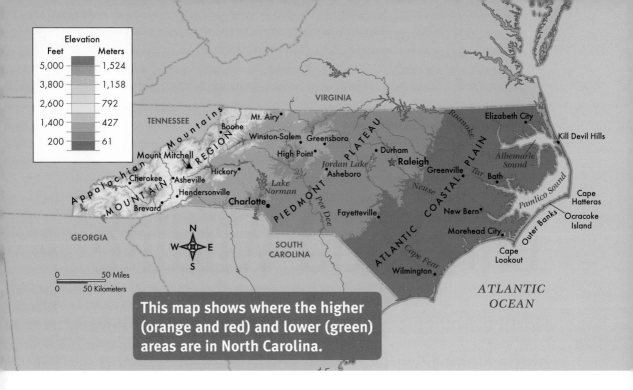

This map shows where the higher (orange and red) and lower (green) areas are in North Carolina.

The Atlantic Coastal Plain

North Carolina measures just over 500 miles (805 km) from east to west. Across that distance, the geography of the state changes dramatically. An area called the Atlantic Coastal Plain covers much of the eastern half of the state. Here the land is flat, the soil is sandy, and the rivers are wide and slow moving. Some of the coastal plain is covered by pine and evergreen forests.

The Outer Banks

The Outer Banks are a line of sandy islands that separate the Atlantic Ocean from mainland North Carolina. In between the islands and the mainland are several large **sounds**. The Outer Banks have beautiful open beaches and a mild **climate** that attract millions of visitors each year. Treacherous seas off the Outer Banks have earned the area the nickname Graveyard of the Atlantic. One of the area's most famous shipwrecks was that of Blackbeard the pirate, whose ship ran aground in 1718.

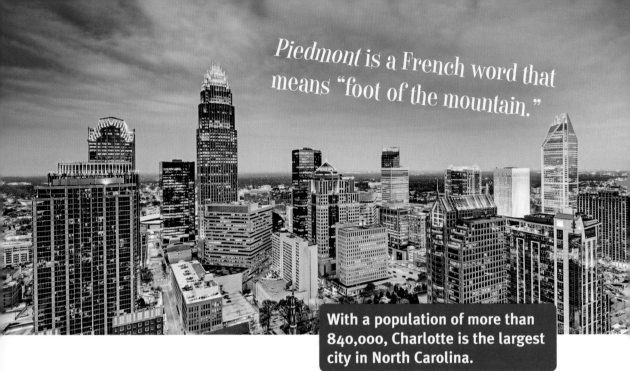

Piedmont is a French word that means "foot of the mountain."

With a population of more than 840,000, Charlotte is the largest city in North Carolina.

The Piedmont

Moving westward from the coastal plain, flat land gives way to the gently rolling hills of the Piedmont region. The Piedmont is North Carolina's most densely populated area. It contains the state's largest cities: Charlotte, Raleigh, Greensboro, and Winston-Salem. In the past, the Piedmont was a center for **agriculture**. But as the cities grew, the area became more focused on business, manufacturing, and industry.

Majestic Mountains

Western North Carolina is a land of dramatic mountain ranges. The Blue Ridge Mountains separate this area from the Piedmont. Some other mountain ranges in North Carolina are the Great Smoky, Pisgah, Balsam, and Bald Mountains. These are all part of the Appalachian Mountains. North Carolina's heavily forested mountain region has numerous streams and more than 300 waterfalls.

Catawba Falls is more than 100 feet (30 m) tall.

The Appalachian Mountains stretch almost 2,000 miles (3,219 km) from Canada to Alabama.

Climate

North Carolina has a varied climate. The warmest part of the state is the central Piedmont, while the coolest temperatures are found in the mountains. North Carolina winters are usually mild. That's because the western mountains block storms and cool air that come in from the Midwest. Coastal North Carolina is often in the path of **hurricanes** that move up from the Caribbean Sea.

MAXIMUM TEMPERATURE
110°F

MINIMUM TEMPERATURE
-34°F

Hurricane winds can cause massive destruction to homes and other buildings.

Water moccasins are also known as cottonmouths.

North Carolina Wildlife

As you'd expect from a state with such varied **habitats**, North Carolina boasts a wide variety of wild animals. The western mountains are home to black bears, bobcats, coyotes, ducks, geese, wild turkeys, and more. Along the coast, you can find alligators and sharks. Reptiles such as turtles, lizards, and snakes are found throughout the state. Some of the most dangerous snakes are rattlesnakes, copperheads, and water moccasins.

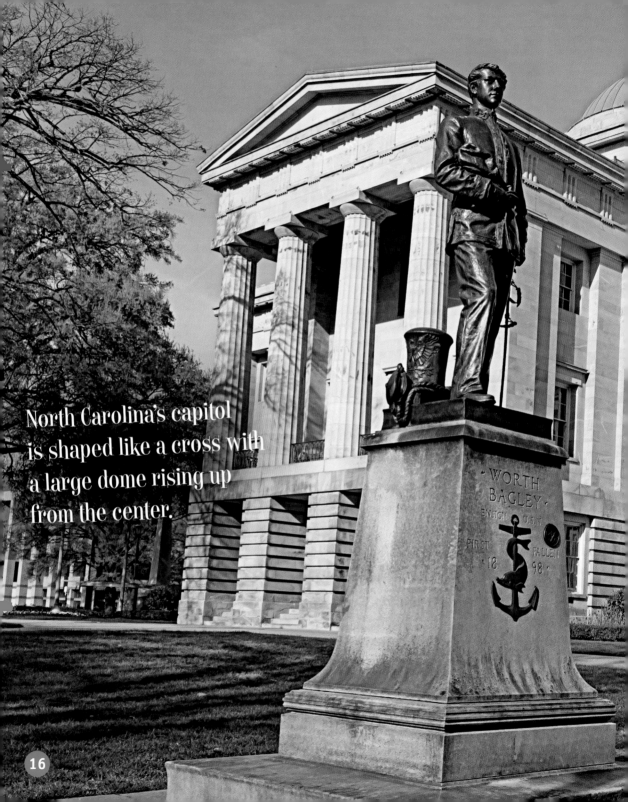

North Carolina's capitol
is shaped like a cross with
a large dome rising up
from the center.

WORTH
BAGLEY
ENSIGN U.S.N
FIRST   FALLEN
· 18   98 ·

CHAPTER 2

Government

In its early years, North Carolina didn't have a capital. The **colony**'s officials met in various places. In 1766, they decided to make New Bern the capital. But once the Revolutionary War started, the town's location made it vulnerable to attack by British troops. As a result, North Carolina's leaders met in several different towns. In 1788, they decided on a permanent location. They voted to purchase land and create a new capital called Raleigh.

Like most other states, North Carolina has a government made up of three branches. The executive branch is headed by the governor. It carries out the laws of the state. The legislative branch's job is to create laws. It is made up of a Senate and a House of Representatives. Together, they form the General Assembly. The judicial branch is North Carolina's court system. It interprets the state's laws.

NORTH CAROLINA'S STATE GOVERNMENT

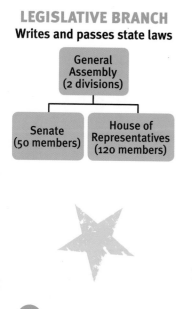

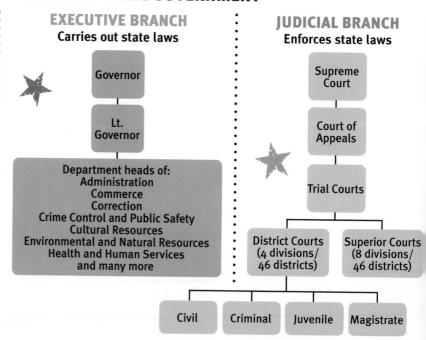

LEGISLATIVE BRANCH
Writes and passes state laws

General Assembly (2 divisions)

Senate (50 members)

House of Representatives (120 members)

EXECUTIVE BRANCH
Carries out state laws

Governor

Lt. Governor

Department heads of:
Administration
Commerce
Correction
Crime Control and Public Safety
Cultural Resources
Environmental and Natural Resources
Health and Human Services
and many more

JUDICIAL BRANCH
Enforces state laws

Supreme Court

Court of Appeals

Trial Courts

District Courts (4 divisions/ 46 districts)

Superior Courts (8 divisions/ 46 districts)

Civil

Criminal

Juvenile

Magistrate

Former North Carolina Attorney General and state legislator Roy Cooper became governor in 2017.

Local Leaders

There are 100 counties in North Carolina. Each has its own local government led by a board of commissioners. There are three to seven members on each board. They are elected by county residents.

Some of the state's towns and cities also have their own separate governments. However, for the hundreds of very small towns spread across North Carolina's rural areas, county leaders are the only form of local government.

North Carolina's National Role

Each state sends elected officials to represent it in the U.S. Congress. Like every state, North Carolina has two senators. The U.S. House of Representatives relies on a state's population to determine its numbers. North Carolina has 13 representatives in the House.

Every four years, states vote on the next U.S. president. Each state is granted a number of electoral votes based on its number of members in Congress. With two senators and 13 representatives, North Carolina has 15 electoral votes.

2 senators and 13 representatives

15 electoral votes

With 15 electoral votes, North Carolina has a strong voice in presidential elections.

Representing North Carolina

Elected officials in North Carolina represent a population with a range of interests, lifestyles, and backgrounds.

Ethnicity (2015 estimates)

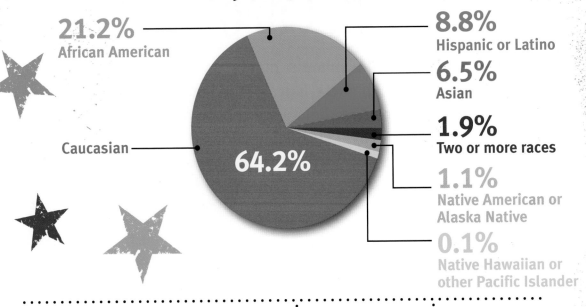

21.2%
African American

8.8%
Hispanic or Latino

6.5%
Asian

1.9%
Two or more races

Caucasian

64.2%

1.1%
Native American or
Alaska Native

0.1%
Native Hawaiian or
other Pacific Islander

85.5% of the population graduated from high school.

7.7% of North Carolinians were born in other countries.

>25% of the population has a degree beyond high school.

15.1% of the population is over 65 years old, and **22.8%** is under 18.

51.3% of the population is female, and **48.7%** is male.

11.2% of North Carolinians speak a language other than English at home.

THE **BIG** TRUTH!

What Represents North Carolina?

States choose specific animals, plants, and objects to represent the values and characteristics of the land and its people. Find out why these symbols were chosen to represent North Carolina or discover surprising curiosities about them.

Seal

North Carolina's state seal shows two figures, Liberty and Plenty, in front of mountains and the ocean. Two historic dates also appear on the seal. On May 20, 1775, the people of Mecklenburg County are said to have declared independence from Great Britain. The Halifax Resolves, issued on April 12, 1776, declared North Carolina's readiness to take action for independence.

Flag

These two important dates also appear on the state flag, which features blue, red, and white bars and the letters N and C on either side of a white star. Until 1885, the flag was slightly different. The lower date was May 20, 1861, the day North Carolina **seceded** from the Union during the Civil War.

Honeybee

STATE INSECT

North Carolinians have long used this insect's honey and wax to make food, medicine, candles, and many other products.

Gray Squirrel

STATE MAMMAL

This tree-dwelling mammal can be found in all 100 of North Carolina's counties.

Emerald

STATE MINERAL

This rare and beautiful green stone is prized for its use in jewelry.

Plott Hound

STATE DOG

This dog is the only officially recognized breed to have developed in North Carolina.

Cardinal

STATE BIRD

In 1943, people all across North Carolina voted on which bird species should represent the state. With about 5,000 votes, the cardinal won.

Sweet Potato

STATE VEGETABLE

This tasty vegetable was first grown in North Carolina by Native Americans centuries ago.

CHAPTER 3

History

In prehistoric times, the entire eastern half of North Carolina was underwater. Historians believe that humans first came to the area between 10,000 and 8000 BCE. These early Native Americans were **nomads**. They hunted large animals for food, gathered wild plants, and may have caught fish and shellfish. But they left no evidence of permanent settlements.

Ancient people in North Carolina hunted large animals that are extinct today.

Settling Down

By about 2000 BCE, Native Americans had begun to create permanent homes. They also cleared fields and started farming. Their crops included gourds, maize, squash, and sunflowers. Eventually, there were about 30 different groups scattered across what is now North Carolina. These included the Cherokee, Waxhaw, Tuscarora, and Catawba. By the mid-1500s CE, before the arrival of European settlers, tens of thousands of Native Americans lived in North Carolina.

This map shows some of the major tribes that lived in what is now North Carolina before Europeans came.

Some experts believe that as many as 90 percent of all Native Americans died of diseases introduced by the Europeans.

Some of North Carolina's Native Americans lived in homes called longhouses.

European Exploration

In 1539, Hernando de Soto, a Spanish explorer, landed near Tampa Bay, Florida. He and his men made their way through Georgia, the Carolinas, and on to Tennessee. Along the way, they met many Native American groups. Some of these meetings were friendly, but many were not. The Europeans brought measles, smallpox, and influenza. These diseases proved deadly to the Native Americans.

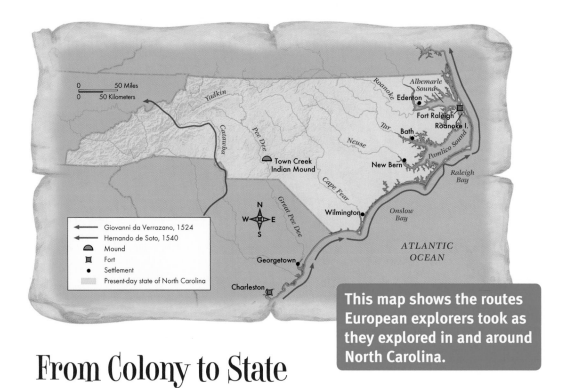

This map shows the routes European explorers took as they explored in and around North Carolina.

From Colony to State

In the 1600s, English colonists from Virginia moved south and settled in the coastal area of North Carolina. The population grew, and in 1663, the king of England granted permission for the area to become a new colony. It would be called Carolina, in honor of his father, Charles I. At first, the colony included land that is now North and South Carolina. However, disputes between the colonists and the colonial government led Carolina to split in two by 1712.

As time went by, the American colonists grew unhappy with British rule. In April 1776, North Carolina became the first of the 13 colonies to vote in favor of independence. The United States was established after the end of the Revolutionary War (1775–1783), and on November 21, 1789, North Carolina officially became the newly formed country's 12th state.

American forces fight Great Britain in the Battle of Guilford Court House, which took place in North Carolina in March 1781.

The Trail of Tears

By the 1820s, many European settlers had moved onto Cherokee lands. The settlers wanted those lands for themselves, so the U.S. government passed a law called the Indian Removal Act. In 1838, U.S. troops began rounding up Cherokees and forcing them to travel to Oklahoma. The route they took became known as the Trail of Tears. Bad weather, disease, and ill treatment by the troops led to the deaths of many people along the way.

Timeline of North Carolina Events

1540
Spanish explorer Hernando de Soto passes through the North Carolina area in search of gold.

1587
John White establishes a second colony at Roanoke Island.

1540

1584

1587

1584
Queen Elizabeth I of England grants permission to Sir Walter Raleigh to colonize America.

Slavery

Like many states, North Carolina participated in the slave trade. People in Africa were captured, taken to America, and forced to work on **plantations**. By 1800, there were 140,000 black people living in North Carolina. Almost all of them were slaves. Many people in the North wanted to end slavery, but those in the South disagreed. This conflict led to the Civil War (1861–1865), and in 1861, North Carolina seceded from the Union.

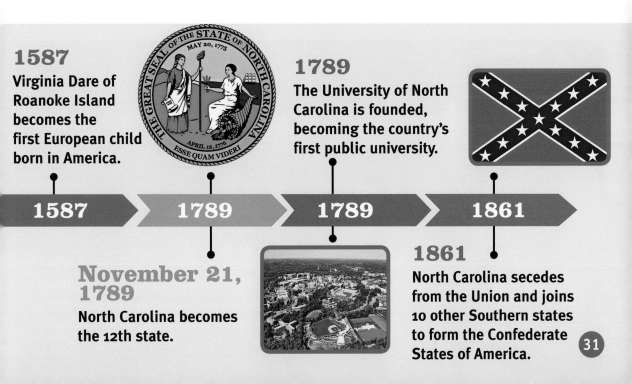

1587
Virginia Dare of Roanoke Island becomes the first European child born in America.

1789
The University of North Carolina is founded, becoming the country's first public university.

| 1587 | 1789 | 1789 | 1861 |

November 21, 1789
North Carolina becomes the 12th state.

1861
North Carolina secedes from the Union and joins 10 other Southern states to form the Confederate States of America.

31

The Civil War had a devastating effect on the country. After it ended in 1865, North Carolina was readmitted to the Union in 1868. The postwar years were hard for the South, but the economy began picking up in the late 1800s.

In the 1950s and 1960s, North Carolina became a center of the civil rights movement. In 1960, four students held the first ever sit-in at a lunch counter in Greensboro. Sit-ins soon became a popular form of resistance against racism across the country.

During their historic sit-in, these African American college students sat down at a whites-only lunch counter and refused to leave until they were served.

The Lost Colony

In 1584, an Englishman named Sir Walter Raleigh sent explorers to America to start a colony. The following year, the first English settlement was established at Roanoke Island, on the coast of North Carolina. The colony soon failed. In 1587, Raleigh sent explorer John White and a group of settlers to start a second colony on Roanoke Island. After starting the colony, White returned to England for supplies. When he came back to Roanoke Island in 1590, there was no sign of the settlers. The entire colony had vanished!

To create pottery, craftspeople shape clay as it spins around on a wheel.

CHAPTER 4

Culture

Traditional crafts such as pottery making, basket making, and metalworking have been a part of North Carolina's culture for centuries. When European settlers arrived, they were introduced to the traditional crafts of Native American tribes living in the area. They traded for baskets and pottery and also developed their own traditions. In the remote mountains of Appalachia, crafting household tools, weaving fabric, and building furniture were necessary parts of life. North Carolina craftspeople still create many beautiful traditional crafts today.

Sports and Recreation

One of the biggest rivalries in college sports is between the men's basketball teams at Duke University and the University of North Carolina (UNC). Among the state's professional sports teams are the Carolina Panthers (football) and the Charlotte Hornets (basketball).

Because of its mild climate and varied **terrain**, North Carolina offers a wide range of outdoor activities. Its beaches are great for surfing, hang gliding, or just relaxing. Fishing and camping are popular pastimes in its many lakes and parks.

Instructors teach a student how to operate a hang glider on an Outer Banks beach.

A traditional bluegrass band performs at Great Smoky Mountains National Park.

Music and Dance

Traditional music and dance play an important role in North Carolina life. The state is especially known for old-time music, a type of folk music that relies heavily on guitar, banjo, fiddle, mandolin, and other stringed instruments. Folk dances such as square dancing and clogging are also popular. Bluegrass music developed in the mountains of Appalachia. It is based on songs and ballads brought by English, Irish, and Scottish settlers.

At Work

While there are several large cities in North Carolina, much of the state remains rural. Agriculture is still a major industry in North Carolina. Its top crops are tobacco and sweet potatoes. In fact, North Carolina produces over half of all sweet potatoes grown in the United States!

A tobacco farmer surveys his crops.

A Technological Wonderland

Today, North Carolina is known for high-tech businesses, some of which are found in an area called the Research Triangle. This area is home to three major universities: Duke, UNC, and North Carolina State University. With so many researchers, scientists, and students nearby, the area has attracted many companies. They work to create the latest technology, medicines, and much more.

North Carolina's Famous Foods

Did you know that Pepsi-Cola and Krispy Kreme Doughnuts got their start in North Carolina? Cheerwine, a soft drink that is distributed throughout the South, was created in the basement of a North Carolina grocery store. Other local specialties include boiled peanuts, pimento cheese, biscuits, and barbecue.

Western North Carolina Barbecue Sauce

Ask an adult to help you!

Ingredients

- 2 cups cider vinegar
- ²/₃ cup ketchup
- ½ cup brown sugar
- 2 tablespoons butter
- 1 tablespoon each of Worcestershire sauce, hot pepper sauce, and lemon juice
- 1 teaspoon each of mustard powder and crushed red pepper flakes
- ½ teaspoon each of salt and pepper

Directions

Place all the ingredients in a saucepan. With an adult's help, bring the sauce to a simmer and cook it over low heat for 30 minutes. Let the sauce cool. Strain it to remove the red pepper flakes. Serve it with barbecued pork, hamburgers, chicken, or whatever you would like!

North Carolina's beaches are a great place to cool off on a hot summer day.

Something for Everyone

Do you enjoy hiking in the mountains, relaxing at the beach, or learning about our nation's history? What about attending a music or dance performance or sitting down to a big plate of barbecue? North Carolina has something to offer everyone. Vibrant cities, beautiful rural areas, and a mild climate are enjoyed by residents and attract visitors all year long. North Carolina may not be a big state, but it has a lot going for it! ★

Famous People

Thomas Wolfe

(1900–1938) was a writer whose works include the novels *Look Homeward, Angel* and *You Can't Go Home Again*. He was born in Asheville.

Thelonious Monk

(1917–1982) was a jazz musician and composer. He played piano and was the second-most recorded jazz composer in history. He was born in Rocky Mount.

Billy Graham

(1918–) is a Christian preacher and religious figure who gave his first sermon on the radio in 1949. Since then, he has reached millions through radio and television. He is from Charlotte.

David Brinkley

(1920–2003) was a newscaster who worked for NBC and ABC. His career lasted over 50 years. He was born in Wilmington.

John Coltrane

(1926–1967) was a famous jazz saxophonist and composer. He was born in Hamlet.

Dale Earnhardt

(1951–2001) was one of the greatest race car drivers in NASCAR history.

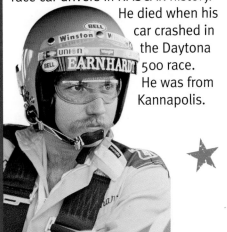

He died when his car crashed in the Daytona 500 race. He was from Kannapolis.

Randy Travis

(1959–) is a singer, songwriter, and musician who has sold over 25 million records. He is from Marshville.

Zach Galifianakis

(1969–) is an actor, writer, and stand-up comedian who has appeared in many hit movies. He is from Wilkesboro.

Julianne Moore

(1960–) is an Academy Award-winning actress who has appeared in such films as *The Lost World: Jurassic Park* and *The Hunger Games* series. She was born in Fayetteville.

Did You Know That ...

Grandfather Mountain boasts the highest peak in the Blue Ridge Mountains and is home to a mile-high swinging bridge.

North Carolina has the largest state-maintained highway system in the United States, with 77,400 miles (124,563 km) of roadways.

Wild ponies run free along the coast of North Carolina. They are the descendants of Spanish mustangs that survived early shipwrecks. Historical research suggests that the first ponies arrived on North Carolina shores as early as 1523.

Biltmore Estate, near Asheville, is the largest privately owned home in the United States.

The University of North Carolina, founded in 1789, is the nation's oldest public university.

Jockey's Ridge is the tallest natural sand dune system in the eastern United States. It is located on North Carolina's Outer Banks.

In the 1700s, one of North Carolina's most important exports was tar. It was a product of the state's abundant pine trees. This helped earn North Carolina its nickname, the Tar Heel State.

Two U.S. presidents were born in North Carolina. James K. Polk was the 11th president, and Andrew Johnson was the 17th.

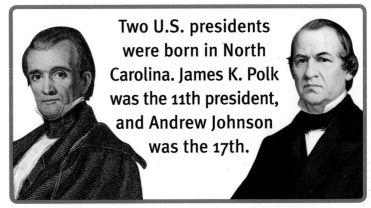

Did you find the truth?

(T) North Carolina fought against the Union during the Civil War.

(F) Sir Walter Raleigh was the first Englishman to visit North Carolina.

Resources

Books

Nonfiction

Heinrichs, Ann. *North Carolina.* New York: Children's Press, 2014.

Otfinoski, Steven. *The Civil War.* New York: Children's Press, 2017.

Fiction

Ransom, Candice F. *Rescue on the Outer Banks.* Minneapolis: Carolrhoda Books, 2002.

Sparks, Nicholas. *A Walk to Remember.* New York: Warner Books, 1999.

Visit this Scholastic website for more information on North Carolina:

 www.factsfornow.scholastic.com
Enter the keywords **North Carolina**

Important Words

agriculture (AG-rih-kuhl-chur) the raising of crops and animals

climate (KLYE-mit) the weather typical of a place over a long period of time

colony (KAH-luh-nee) a community settled in a new land but with ties to another government

habitats (HAB-uh-tats) places or types of places where a plant or animal naturally or normally lives or grows

hurricanes (HUR-uh-kaynz) storms with very strong, destructive winds that rotate

nomads (NOH-madz) people who have no fixed home but wander from place to place

plantations (plan-TAY-shuhnz) large farms where crops such as cotton and tobacco are grown

seceded (sih-SEED-id) formally withdrew from a group or an organization, often to form another organization

sounds (SOWNDZ) long, broad inlets of the ocean generally parallel to the coast

terrain (tuh-RAYN) the physical features of an area of land

Index

Page numbers in **bold** indicate illustrations.

About the Author

Ann O. Squire is a psychologist and an animal behaviorist. Before becoming a writer, she studied the behaviors of rats, tropical fish in the Caribbean, and electric fish from central Africa. Her favorite part of being a writer is the chance to learn as much as she can about all sorts of topics. In addition to *North Carolina*, Dr. Squire has written books about many types of animals, as well as health, earth science, planets, and weather. She lives in Asheville, North Carolina.